Slim Goodbody's Life Skills 101

PAST TENSE

Healthy Ways to Manage Stress

CRABTREE
Publishing Company
www.crabtreebooks.com

Crabtree Publishing Company
www.crabtreebooks.com

Series Development, Writing, and Packaging:
John Burstein, Slim Goodbody Corp.

Editors:
Lynn Peppas
Valerie Weber, Wordsmith Ink.

Editorial director:
Kathy Middleton

Production coordinator:
Ken Wright

Prepress technician:
Ken Wright

Designer:
Tammy West, Westgraphix LLC.

Photos:
Chris Pinchback, Pinchback Photography

"Slim Goodbody" and Pinchback photos, copyright,
© Slim Goodbody

Photo credits:
© Creative Commoms: page 10
© iStock Photos: pages 1 (right), 2, 7, 9, 11,
   14 (bottom right), 15, 17, 19 (top), 24,
   25 (bottom), 26 (top)
© Shutterstock: pages 5
© Slim Goodbody: pages 1 (left), 4, 6, 8, 12, 13,
   14 (top, bottom left), 16, 18, 19 (bottom), 20, 21,
   22, 23, 25 (top, middle), 26 (bottom), 27, 28, 29

Acknowledgements:
The author would like to thank the following
people for their help in this project:
Christine Burstein, Lucas Burstein, Tristan Fong,
Jessie Goodale, Adriana Goodale, Colby Hill, Ginny
Laurita, Louis Laurita, Renaissance Lyman, Jack
Henry Grannis-Phoenix, Ariel Power, Joah Welt

"Slim Goodbody" and "Slim Goodbody's Life
Skills 101" are registered trademarks of the Slim
Goodbody Corp.

Library and Archives Canada Cataloguing in Publication

Burstein, John
    Past tense : healthy ways to manage stress / John Burstein.

(Slim Goodbody's life skills 101)
Includes index.
Issued also in an electronic format.
ISBN 978-0-7787-4796-3 (bound).--ISBN 978-0-7787-4812-0 (pbk.)

    1. Stress management--Juvenile literature. 2. Stress
(Psychology)--Juvenile literature. I. Title. II. Title: Healthy
ways to manage stress. III. Series: Burstein, John. Slim
Goodbody's life skills 101.

RA785.B87 2011   j155.9'042   C2010-902763-9

Library of Congress Cataloging-in-Publication Data

Burstein, John.
    Past tense : healthy ways to manage stress / [John Burstein].
       p. cm. -- (Slim Goodbody's life skills 101)
    Includes index.
    ISBN 978-0-7787-4812-0 (pbk. : alk. paper) -- ISBN 978-0-7787-4796-3
(reinforced library binding : alk. paper) -- ISBN 978-1-4271-9534-0
(electronic (pdf))
    1. Stress management for children--Juvenile literature. 2. Stress in children--
Juvenile literature. I. Title. II. Series.

    RA785.B88 2011
    616.9'8008--dc22
                                                         2010016404

Crabtree Publishing Company

www.crabtreebooks.com   1-800-387-7650

Printed in China/082010/AP20100512

Published in Canada
Crabtree Publishing
616 Welland Ave.
St. Catharines, Ontario
L2M 5V6

Published in the United States
Crabtree Publishing
PMB 59051
350 Fifth Avenue, 59th Floor
New York, New York 10118

Published in the United Kingdom
Crabtree Publishing
Maritime House
Basin Road North, Hove
BN41 1WR

Published in Australia
Crabtree Publishing
386 Mt. Alexander Rd.
Ascot Vale (Melbourne)
VIC 3032

CONTENTS

LEFT OUT? 4

WHAT CAUSES STRESS? 6

SIGNS OF STRESS 8

A LITTLE HISTORY LESSON 10

STRESS RESPONSE 12

POSITIVE STRESS 14

TOO MUCH IS TOO MUCH 16

TAKE ACTION–SKILL ONE:
   CHECK YOUR STRESS 18

SKILL TWO: TALK IT OUT 20

SKILLS THREE, FOUR, AND FIVE 21

SKILL SIX: LEARN TO RELAX 22

DEEP BREATHING 24

USE YOUR IMAGINATION 26

SKILL SEVEN:
   TREAT YOUR BODY WELL 27

STAY POSITIVE 28

GLOSSARY 30

FOR MORE INFORMATION 31

INDEX 32

Words in **bold** are defined in the glossary on page 30.

LEFT OUT?

Ashley was in the lunch line at school. "I'm so hungry, I could eat a horse," she said.

"I think that's what they're serving today," joked her friend Kayla. Ashley started laughing. Then Kayla asked, "What are you giving Brian for his birthday on Saturday?"

All of a sudden, Ashley stopped laughing. She felt a knot start to form in her stomach. She hadn't been invited to the party, but she didn't want Kayla to know that! So she said, "I have to think about it. What are you giving him?"

As Kayla talked, Ashley couldn't focus on what was being said. Too many worried thoughts were flying around in her head. "I thought Brian was my friend. What's the matter with me? Did I do anything wrong? I'm so embarrassed."

Ashley started to feel hot. She was even beginning to sweat. She turned to Kayla and said, "I'm not feeling so well. I think I'll skip lunch."

"I thought you were starving," replied Kayla.

"I was, but not any more. Maybe I should see the nurse," said Ashley as she walked away.

At the door of the lunchroom, Brian came over to Ashley. He said, "Hi! I've been looking for you. Would you like to come to my birthday party this Saturday?"

Ashley smiled and said, "Thanks, Brian, I'd love to."

When Brian walked away, Ashley thought, "This is so weird. A minute ago I was feeling sick. Now I'm feeling wonderful. How is that possible?"

Hi. My name is Slim Goodbody.

When you are faced with certain upsetting **situations**, a series of amazing changes happen inside your body. These changes can cause you to feel very tense. This tension is called stress.

Everyone feels stress from time to time. I wrote this book to teach you about what happens inside your body when you face stressful situations. You'll also learn skills to deal with stress and ways to avoid feeling stress. Knowing how to recognize and manage stress will help you lead a happier and healthier life.

WHAT CAUSES STRESS?

Stress can be caused by events that happen to you. People around you can also stress you. Plus, the pressure you put on yourself causes stress.

Situations that lead to stress are called **stressors**. Stressors make you feel frightened, worried, angry, or upset. Examples include

- taking a surprise quiz
- getting a lot of homework
- getting lost
- feeling hungry
- being bullied
- going to a party where you don't know many people
- almost getting into an accident
- having a parent or friend yell at you
- changing schools in the middle of the year
- being in a thunderstorm when the lights go out
- playing in an important ball game
- seeing a stranger walking toward you
- having an injury or illness

Not every stressor affects everyone in the same way. Some people become angry. Some people become very quiet and hold their feelings in. Some people can't focus. Some people even get sick.

Serious Stress

You may have heard of a problem called post-traumatic stress disorder. This serious illness is caused by severe stressors. For example, people can develop post-traumatic stress disorder if they have

- fought in a war;
- been involved in a serious accident;
- experienced the death of a loved one;
- been caught in a natural disaster.

Post-traumatic stress disorder is not a normal kind of stress. People with post-traumatic stress disorder need to be treated by doctors.

SIGNS OF STRESS

It is important to learn the warning signs of stress. Sometimes the signs can be **physical** and affect the way your body works. Sometimes the signs can be **mental** and affect the way you think and feel. Usually when you feel stress, there will be a combination of physical and mental signs.

Here are the most common signs of stress:

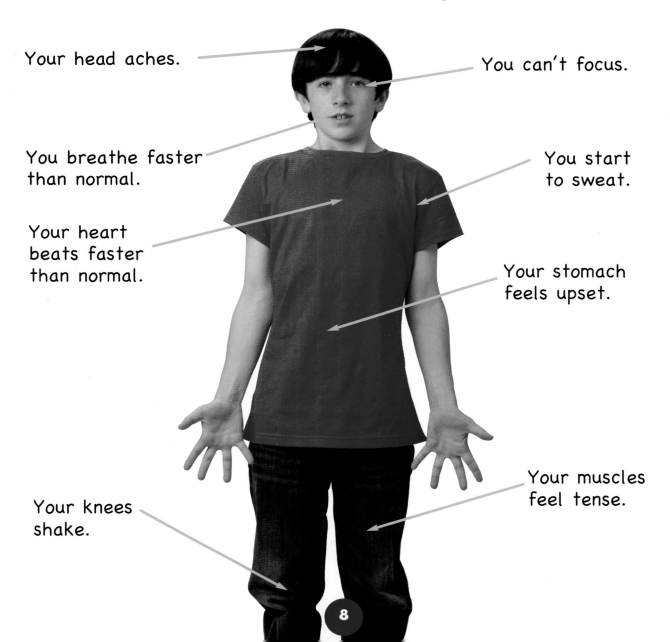

Your head aches.

You can't focus.

You breathe faster than normal.

You start to sweat.

Your heart beats faster than normal.

Your stomach feels upset.

Your muscles feel tense.

Your knees shake.

Delayed Reaction

Sometimes something happens that causes stress, but you don't notice any physical or mental **reactions** right away. Later on, however, you find that

- you become very sad and moody;
- you can't get a good night's sleep;
- you lose your appetite;
- your stomach hurts;
- you have an **allergy** attack, or your **asthma** gets worse;
- you lose interest in school.

These are examples of delayed reactions to stress.

How Stress Spreads

Stress affects the people around you. For example, if you are feeling stress, you may yell at your family or friends. But in your heart, you might not be angry with them at all. You may not even be aware of how you are behaving. However, they may think you are mad at them because your behavior seems mean or rude. Not only that, your behavior can cause stress in someone else. Understanding when you are feeling stress can help you learn not to take it out on others.

A LITTLE HISTORY LESSON

Stress began as a tool for survival. It has been a part of the human experience for thousands of years. To really understand how and why stress was so important, let's take a brief trip back in time—to **prehistoric** days.

Imagine that you and your family lived in a cave and gathered seeds and nuts for food. One day, you were out looking for food. Suddenly, you looked up and saw a **saber-toothed tiger** closing in on you. You were about to become a meal yourself! This kind of danger caused a lot of stress.

There were only two things you could do to stay alive. You could either fight—or run away. In either case, your body had to get ready quickly. To do that, changes began to happen in your body. These changes caused extra energy to flow to your muscles. You became faster and stronger. Your eyesight and hearing became sharper.

If you were forced to fight, these physical changes helped you do a better job. If you tried to run away, you could move a lot more quickly. Scientists call these changes the fight-or-**flight** response or the **stress response**.

Saber-tooths Die Out, Fight or Flight Remains

Of course, times have changed. People today are rarely in situations where they need to fight or run away. Most of the stressful situations you face aren't likely to end with you becoming a meal. In modern life, there aren't a lot of animal attacks! But that fact doesn't change what happens inside you. Your fight-or-flight response still kicks in when you are faced with stressful situations.

STRESS RESPONSE

When the fight-or-flight response kicks in, some amazing things begin to happen inside of your body.

- First, your nervous system gets into gear. Your senses report information to your brain. Your brain now knows you may be in danger.

- Next, a part of your brain called the hypothalamus releases chemical messengers into the blood flowing through your body. These messengers are called **hormones**.

- The hormones flow to a nearby **gland** called the pituitary gland. They cause the pituitary gland to release other hormones into your blood.

- These hormones travel down to your adrenal glands. The adrenal glands release hormones called adrenaline and cortisol into your bloodstream.

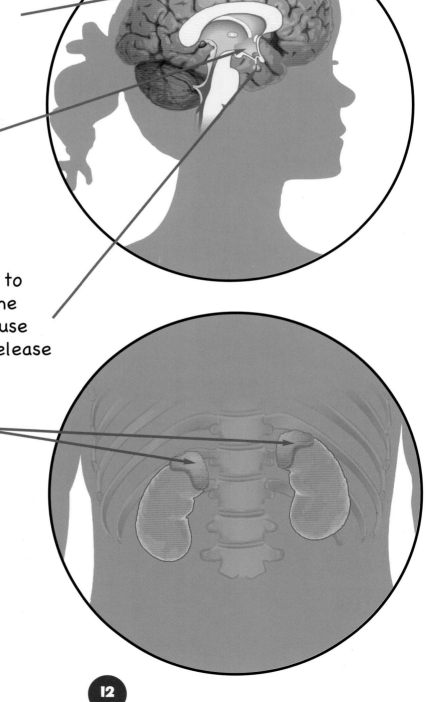

• Adrenaline and cortisol flow through your body and speed up your heart rate. Your heart rate is how many times your heart beats in a minute. Your increased heart rate moves the blood around your body more quickly.

• Your breathing gets faster, so you take in more **oxygen** from the air around you.

• Your liver releases some of its stored sugars. (By the way, this isn't the same sugar as you get from soft drinks, candy, and cookies! You don't need that sugar to help your fight-or-flight response!) The added oxygen and sugar allow your **cells** to make more energy. You can use this energy to run away from trouble or fight off an attacking animal.

• Adrenaline and cortisol also cause your **blood vessels** to open wider. The wider openings let more blood flow to large muscle groups. Extra blood gives your muscles more strength and quicker reaction time.

• The pupils in your eyes dilate. Dilating means they get wide to improve your vision.

• Your hearing gets sharper.

All of these physical changes get you ready to perform well under pressure.

POSITIVE STRESS

Many people think that stress is always negative and bad for you. That is not true. There are many positive effects of stress. Stress can help keep you safe or even save your life in an emergency. Suppose you're riding your bike and a cat jumps out in front of you. The stress can speed up your reaction time so you slam on the brakes faster to avoid an accident.

14

Eustress

Stress can also be helpful when there's no actual danger, but there is pressure to do something well. Scientists call this kind of stress eustress.

When you need to do something that takes a little extra strength and focus, eustress kicks in. For example, soccer players can gain strength and speed from eustress right before they play a big game. A basketball player can get help from eustress when stepping up to take a foul shot that could win the game. Eustress can also give you a little extra push that can help you prepare well for a test or play a part on stage. Eustress helps you give a better speech in front of your class.

A little eustress can help keep you on your toes. It helps you rise to a challenge or handle a tough situation. Eustress increases your focus, strength, and alertness.

Shut Off

The changes in your body from eustress continue until the challenge is met. Once the situation is over, the stress response usually cuts off. The hormones stop flowing through you. Your muscles relax, and your breathing and heart rate slow down. Your body quickly returns to its normal state. You become calm but ready to respond to the next challenge when it arises.

TOO MUCH IS TOO MUCH

A little stress may be positive, but too much stress isn't good for anyone. For example, you may feel a little stress about an upcoming test. That small amount of stress can make you want to study hard. But stressing out for days and days before the exam can make you too wound up to focus.

Over and Over

Sometimes stressful situations must be faced over and over again. For example,

- You are having trouble with math. Every time you go to math class, you feel stress. You feel the same way when you do your math homework later.

- A bully lives near your home. Every day you have to face the bully on your way to and from school.

- You move to a new school and have a hard time making friends.

- Your parents are going through a divorce and seem to argue all the time.

- Your family worries over money problems at home.

Stressful situations like these can cause real troubles. Since you keep getting upset, your body doesn't have a chance to fully relax and get back to normal. Stress hormones keep getting released into your blood. After a while, your energy gets used up.

The stressful situation doesn't go away, but your body becomes too tired to handle it. If the stress continues for too long, it can affect nearly every system in your body. It can weaken your **immune system** and increase the risk of heart disease.

TAKE ACTION

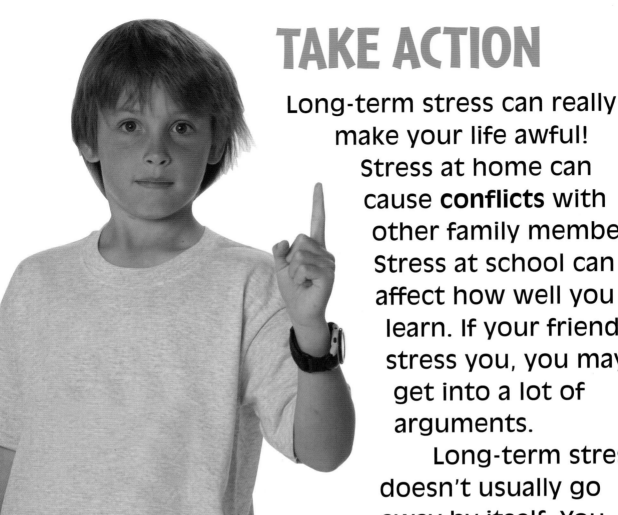

Long-term stress can really make your life awful! Stress at home can cause **conflicts** with other family members. Stress at school can affect how well you learn. If your friends stress you, you may get into a lot of arguments.

Long-term stress doesn't usually go away by itself. You must deal with it.

Dealing with it means you can't ignore it or run away from it. Luckily there are skills you can practice to learn to manage and reduce your stress.

Skill One: Check Your Stress

The first step in dealing with stress is to understand what causes you to feel stressed out. Understanding your stress will help you figure out how to deal with it. Ask yourself, "What makes me feel stress?"

Think about It

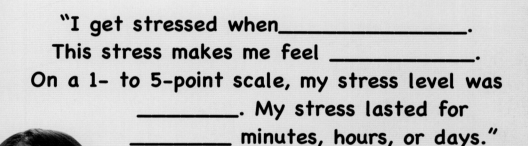

It will probably help to think about what has happened in your life during the past few weeks. Try to remember times when you got tense, worried, upset, angry, or frightened. Write down your answers in a Stress Notebook using this formula:

"I get stressed when_____.
This stress makes me feel _____.
On a 1- to 5-point scale, my stress level was
_____. My stress lasted for
_____ minutes, hours, or days."

Remember that in this scale, one means you're feeling very little stress. The highest number, five, means you're totally stressed out.

Try to be as detailed as possible. Do you feel the stress in your head, your stomach, your muscles, or some other part of your body? Was your stress mild or serious?

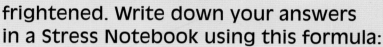

SKILL TWO: TALK IT OUT

Once you understand more about the stress you feel, you can start to take some action. One of the best things you can do is to talk things out. Explain your feelings to a parent, teacher, or friend. Ask for help if you feel the stress is too much to handle alone.

Many times talking things through will help you see new ways to handle tough situations. You'll feel more confident and less stressed.

Skill Three: Befriend Yourself

Be a good friend to yourself. When you start to feel stress, remind yourself of some of the things below:

- The stressful situation will not last forever.
- I am a good, strong person.
- I am smart enough to handle most stressful situations.

- I know how to ask for help if I need it.
- I deserve to have good things happen.

Skill Four: Stay Away from Stress

Do your best to avoid situations you know will be stressful. For example, if you feel stress because you usually wait until the last minute to do your homework, start it earlier.

Skill Five: Be Realistic

Not all stress comes from things that happen to you. Sometimes your own way of thinking can add to your stress. For example, some people get stressed if they don't do things perfectly. It is fine to set high standards for yourself, but nobody is perfect. Everyone makes mistakes. All you can do is your very best. Remind yourself that that is enough.

SKILL SIX: LEARN TO RELAX

Your body has a built-in ability to deal with stress. This ability is called the relaxation response. The relaxation response is the opposite of the fight-or-flight response. It brings your body back into balance. The relaxation response

- reduces stress hormones;
- slows your heart rate and breathing;
- releases muscle tension;
- improves concentration.

Several kinds of relaxation exercises will help you tap into the relaxation response. I'm going to teach you three of these exercises. Pick whichever one you think will work best for you.

Progressive Muscle Relaxation

Progressive muscle relaxation is a two-step process. First you focus on making different parts of your body tense. Then you focus on completely relaxing those parts. Here are the steps:

- Loosen any tight clothes. Take off your shoes. Lay down on your bed or on a couch.

- Breathe in and out slowly. Take about five nice deep breaths.

- Focus your attention on your left foot. Squeeze all the foot muscles together as tightly as you can. Hold for a count of ten.

- Relax your left foot. Feel the tension flowing away. Feel your foot become loose and fully relaxed.

- Shift your attention to your right foot. Tense and fully relax the foot the same way you did with your left foot.

- Move slowly up through your body. Tense and relax each muscle group as you move up. Move through your left calf, right calf, left thigh, right thigh, hips and buttocks, stomach, chest, back, left arm, left hand, right arm, right hand, neck, shoulders, and face. The next time you start feeling tense, you will have a tool to help you begin to relax right away.

DEEP BREATHING

Deep breathing is a simple and powerful way to relax. It's easy to learn. It can be practiced almost anywhere, and it provides a quick way to calm down. All you need is a few minutes and a place to stretch out.

Most people take shallow breaths. They just fill the top part of their lungs. The key to deep breathing is filling your lungs fully without straining. To do this, you need to breathe from your abdomen instead of just your chest. It may help to compare deep breathing to filling a glass with water. The water fills up the bottom of the glass first. Then the water rises up to the top.

During deep breathing, you want something similar to happen in your lungs. You want the air to fill the bottom of your lungs first. As you keep breathing, the air fills the middle and top of your lungs.

Here is how deep breathing is done:

- Put your hands on your stomach.

- Exhale, trying to empty all the air from your lungs.

- Breathe in slowly through your nose to a count of five. The hands on your stomach should rise before your chest begins to move.

- Breathe out slowly through your mouth to a count of five. Push out as much air as you can by pulling in your abdominal muscles. The hands on your stomach should move in as you exhale.

- Continue to breathe in through your nose and out through your mouth for ten to fifteen minutes.

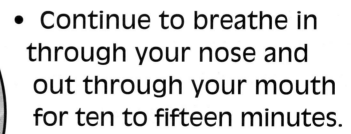

USE YOUR IMAGINATION

Another helpful relaxation exercise involves your imagination. Begin by choosing a peaceful scene to imagine. It might be by the ocean or taking a stroll in a beautiful meadow. Choose whatever place feels most calming to you. Here are the steps to take:

1. Sit in a quiet spot and loosen any tight clothing.

2. Close your eyes and imagine your restful place.

3. Picture your place with as much detail as possible. Try to use all your senses. For example, if you are imagining sitting by a quiet lake,

- **see** the sun shining on the water;
- **hear** the birds singing;

- **smell** the nearby pine trees;
- **feel** the cool water on your bare feet;
- **taste** the fresh, clean air.

Spend about ten to fifteen minutes imagining. Then slowly open your eyes and come back to the real world.

Skill Seven: Treat Your Body Well

The healthier you are, the better you will be able to manage stress. Here are some of the most important things you can do to treat your body well:

- **Exercise** is a great stress reliever. As you exercise, your muscles release tension. You also tend to stop thinking about your problems.

- **Stretching** helps relax tense muscles. Hold each stretch for ten seconds or longer. Be gentle and don't overstretch.

- **Eat well** to help your body get the fuel it needs to work at its best. Avoid sugary foods that fill you up without providing the **nutrients** you need. Avoid soft drinks that contain **caffeine**.

- **Get enough sleep** to help keep your body and mind in top shape. When you are feeling awake and aware, you can deal better with stressful situations.

STAY POSITIVE

Scientists have discovered that a lot of stress-fighting ability has to do with attitude. For example, people who deal well with stress

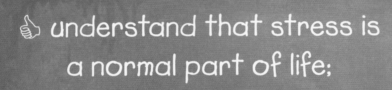

👍 understand that stress is a normal part of life;

👍 think of problems as challenges, not disasters;

👍 see challenges as temporary;

👍 take action when faced with challenges;

👍 believe in their ability to succeed.

Keep Practicing

You've learned a lot about stress. You know what causes it and what happens to you inside. You also know what steps to take to reduce stress in your life. But knowledge alone is not enough. You need to put what you know into practice. Remember to use the skills you've learned:

SKILL ONE: CHECK YOUR STRESS

SKILL TWO: TALK IT OUT

SKILL THREE: BEFRIEND YOURSELF

SKILL FOUR: STAY AWAY FROM STRESS

SKILL FIVE: BE REALISTIC

SKILL SIX: LEARN TO RELAX

SKILL SEVEN: TREAT YOUR BODY WELL

Now You Know

The better you are able to manage stress, the happier and healthier you will be. But don't let your efforts to deal with stress cause you to feel more stress! Be patient with yourself. It takes time to make changes. Believe in yourself. You are sure to succeed.

GLOSSARY

allergy A strong reaction to something breathed in, tasted, or touched that quickly causes itching, rashes, or sneezing

asthma A lung disease that causes breathing problems

blood vessels Small tubes in the body through which blood travels

caffeine A bitter substance in many coffees and teas; it gives people energy for a short time

cells Tiny units that are the basic building blocks of all living things

conflicts Strong disagreements or fights

flight The act of running away

gland A part of the body that makes special chemicals needed for the body to work properly

hormones Chemicals made in the body that help it grow or stay healthy. Glands make hormones, which travel through the body in the blood.

immune system All of the parts of the body that join together to fight off diseases

mental Done by or having to do with the mind

nutrients Chemical compounds (such as protein and vitamins) that make up foods. The body uses nutrients to function and grow.

oxygen An invisible gas in the air that animals need to live

physical Having to do with the body

prehistoric Describes ancient times long ago before people could write things down

progressive Moving forward

reactions Changes in response to something happening

saber-toothed tiger A prehistoric, large animal from the cat family with long sharp teeth

situations The way things are; conditions

stressors People, events, or things that make someone feel stress

stress response Changes in your body when danger threatens or a tense situation occurs

BOOKS

Culbert, Timothy, M.D. and Rebecca Kajander C.P.N.P. M.P.H. *Be the Boss of Your Stress: Self-Care for Kids*. Free Spirit Publishing

Huebner, Dawn. *What to Do When You Worry Too Much: A Kid's Guide to Overcoming Anxiety*. Magination Press

Lite, Lori. *Bubble Riding: A Relaxation Story*. Stress Free Kids

Romain, Trevor and Elizabeth Verdick. *Stress Can Really Get on Your Nerves!* Free Spirit Publishing

WEB SITES

BAM: Body and Mind
www.bam.gov/sub_yourlife/yourlife_stressometer.html
Take the "stress-o-meter" quiz to find out all about your level of stress. Then search for the "Feelin' Frazzled" link to find activities that will help reduce your stress.

KidsHealth
http://kidshealth.org/kid/feeling/emotion/stress.html
This wonderful, kid-friendly site will help you learn more about stress and finding ways to relax.

Kids' Health
www.cyh.com/HealthTopics/HealthTopicDetailsKids.aspx?p=335&np=287&id=1738
This fun and informative site helps children learn about what causes stress and how to relax.

Slim Goodbody
www.slimgoodbody.com
Discover loads of fun and free downloads for kids, teachers, and parents.

INDEX

Adrenal glands 12
Allergies 9
Appetite 9
Asthma 9
Attitudes 28
Avoiding stress 5, 21

Blood 12, 13, 17
Brain 12
Breathing 8, 13, 15, 22, 23, 24–25

Cells 13

Dealing with stress 5, 18-27, 28, 29
Delayed reactions to stress 9

Eating 27
Effects of stress 4, 5, 7, 8, 9, 10, 11, 12–13, 14, 15, 16, 17, 18
Eustress 15
Events causing stress 4, 5, 6, 10, 11, 16, 17,
   See also Stressors
Exercise 27
Eyesight 8, 10, 13

Feelings 7, 8, 9, 18,19, 20
Fight or flight response 10, 11, 12–13, 15, 22
Focus 4, 7, 8, 15, 16, 22, 23

Head 4, 8, 19
Hearing 10, 13

Heart 8, 13, 15, 17, 22
Hormones 12, 13, 15, 17, 22
Hypothalamus 12

Imagination and stress 26–27
Immune system 17

Liver 13

Muscles 8, 10, 13, 15, 19, 22, 23, 25, 27

People causing stress 4, 6, 9, 17, 18
Pituitary gland 12
Positive stress 14, 15
Post-traumatic stress disorder 7
Prehistoric days 10

Relaxation response 22, 23, 24–25, 26–27

Saber-toothed tigers 10, 11
Sleeping 9, 27
Stomach 4, 8, 9, 19, 25
Stress response, See Fight or flight response
Stressors 6–7
Stretching 27
Sugars 13
Sweating 4, 8

Talking about stress 20

About the Author

John Burstein (also known as Slim Goodbody) has been entertaining and educating children for over thirty years. His programs have been broadcast on CBS, PBS, Nickelodeon, USA, and Discovery. He has won numerous awards including the Parent's Choice Award and the President's Council's Fitness Leader Award. Currently, Mr. Burstein tours the country with his multimedia live show "Bodyology." For more information, please visit **slimgoodbody.com**.